I ʃɪɑɩ ɩɩ ɪɪɪɛɛɪ yɔʋ
at CUUB!

Happy Poetry
Month —

Terry

Maumee, Maumee

TERRY BLACKHAWK

Alice Greene & Co.
Ann Arbor, Michigan

Alice Greene & Co.
P. O. Box 7406
Ann Arbor, MI 48107
www.alicegreene.com

ISBN 978-1-935770-28-2

Editor: Jill Peek
Cover & Illustrations: Neil Frankenhauser,
permission of Heidi Frankenhauser
Book Design: Colin O'Brien

Printed in the United States of America

in memoriam

Neil Paul Frankenhauser (1939-2019)

...the purpose of death is the release of love.

– Laurie Anderson

Visitation

Hello, Swallowtail. Hello, companion.
Two days dallying, is that enough?
We both know these flowers will not last.

Hello, fog, hello, rain.
Hello simplicity. Do stop in.

I haven't tried your ladder
in a while. Is its bucket
still there? You know,
the blue one. I'm going to sit
right here on this patch of lawn
cupping my hands until something
lands. Or speaks.

Hello, dear meddler.
You mentioned the news
stopped by.

Tell me everything.

Query

Where do you come from? asked the bridge.
I won't know until I cross you

I replied. I've nothing to lose
by touching down. Softly. Breathless.

Loose petals now. More carpet than
cloud, these ardor-strewn peonies.

Every time the moon rises full
it's love's face I see, shining there.

Maumee, Maumee

Fish leap and splash, grasses' heads toss in the wind,
the bowed-over, weighted-down willows swish and sigh,
and the river itself moment by moment, now rippled now
smooth with its swoop of swallows, traffic from the bridge
an endless roar of sea—Maumee, Maumee. I sing it, oriole
hopping from branch to branch, small leaf cutter on the edge
of my page, fingers stained with the green of an oil pastel,
house finch weaving its song, song sparrow cranking up in
the understory. I sing the warble rush flow gritting of teeth
orange truck rushing past the nothing that is here except
these gnats dancing in front of my eyes. I am long gone water
from the bottle, orgasmic fizz, tornado at night passing us
by. I wade the water, but do not go in, so yes Payne's Gray's
a kind of bluish black excellent for painting stormy skies,
and yes, sun sparkle, flashes of dilatory bobble *Flish!* a fish
flips up from the surface. Smooth the paint on the panel,
sweetie, dive, won't you? And don't argue. My tone is your
tone your town your tongue. Kayaks floating past and Sunday
afternoons by our own *Grande Jatté*. Pigeons that fly up. The
necessary dark.

No notes, just the way
that warbler bounced and climbed each
available twig.

In Duple Time

Czardas! On the radio. Bows strike strings
and I learn Tchaikovsky's pledge—twelve "scenes,"
one per month—was not in homage to his muse
but a job, a chore—so unlike your *plein air* duty
to your river where floods have subsided and ice
scarred the bank across the shore. Write a poem
about you? *Amore,* I started to say, *you can't order
a poem*—as if no poem exists without you now
and the hours don't say only your name. *Czardas!*
—a Hungarian tune in a minor key. I discover it's
a wedding dance, after you are gone. The couple
starts slowly then, in duple time, ends with a rapid
whirl. Put those shadows in your painting, darling.
Must we live twice in order to love once?

Of Course

Of course you are not here
                              but you left me
these tilted telephone poles
from the 1920s, a car I can almost
see, and a triangular warning sign
in bright red contrast to the deep
ochre and cobalt shadows crossing
the center line of the road.
It could be the way your dusky trees
in the background swell against
the horizon, amorphous there beyond
the vanishing point—which is of course
where you are now   or almost
on the verge of taking your last breath—
but this road you gave me led me
                  into sleep so often
I'll go down it now   keeping track
and of course   also   not.
This garage on the right—I could pull into it
on an ordinary day, find perhaps a path
alongside, and a bungalow
a few paces ahead, its porch
half hidden by bushes. I'll meet you there.
There must have been some ocean
in the air the day you painted this,
maybe that's why the trees rise and fall
like waves and the sidewalk's edges
seem so liquid, almost ebb and flow.

At the National Gallery of Art: Memorial View

To reach the Rothkos, climb four flights up,
past the Calder floating in light from windows
angled above the terrazzo staircase. Marble bright,
marble light: trilobites and shells embedded
underfoot, and on I go, my river's shores
opening out. I've passed the Bellows you loved,
Hughie Lee-Smith's ghetto flute ascending.

First stop, Magritte: a curtained emptiness.
Next, Max Ernst's "Moment of Calm" belies its name
with a textural busy-ness you'd have defied
these new motion sensors to peer into. I imagine you
imbibing this forest of drowned roller coasters, sgraffito
birds, bristlecone pines, collapsible cups un-collapsing
upward. You always did like to come nose-close.

In my wallet, a profile cut-out: you, hands
thrust in your painting smock, face tilting up,
lips puckered for a kiss—the photo just one
of many surprises you'd tuck into a pocket
or sock drawer before driving back to Toledo.
You may never find this, you wrote on one,
but I hope it brings you joy if you do.

So when I arrive at the Rothkos and start writing
and a stranger interrupts to tell me I'm his "muse,"
I startle. He is so not you, yet I go on, into the Not-you,
blab about Twombley, "art pilgrimages"— but why
talk to him at all? I sought a chapel. Not this.
The black square floats inside the maroon, the red above
the white. None (*all!*) of it is still.

Diptych

i. Drawing You In

A leaf blinks and *voilá*—eyelashes, fins, and scales take shape.
    Call it a banana stuck in a stanza, or a moray stuck
in an eel—I see them in all your river-studies now, lumbering
    quadrupeds, dozy reptiles lying in wait for your doodling
on watercolors you were almost ready to throw away. You trusted
    the toothy paper to snag whatever insisted on being

itself: offbeat fauna emerging from the water—*so hard to paint,*
    yet you did it so well—water that was the paint that was
the river that was the paper in front of you as you sat beside it—
    your Maumee, "sacred" you called it. Mornings, afternoons,
hours spent looking south and east to where the river widened
    then turned toward Lake Erie and then to the sea—

not to the west with its overpass, traffic, Mad Anthony's
    battlefield—*you painted those, too*—or the riverside
camp where the Odawa sheltered runaways from slavery,
    the Great Black Swamp's centuries-old drainage
seeping up now through the wild watershed of history with you
    lost in it. And across the road, the cemetery. Oh, I know

no easy equivalents between outside and in: the wheel turns,
    creatures subside into the leaves and waves they came from,
but if your calling it *sacred* makes it so, maybe I'll plant myself
    there, not far from the water, among the modest stones—
though before I do, grant me just one grain of the sustenance
    that kept you there—drawing you in, drawing you out.

ii. Singing You Up

Today I cannot fathom news from the waves
or the calendar established by the bees,
but something in the moon last night waxing
for the fifth time since you died, with planets

in their astonishing alignment, has me reaching
across miles, not to your house, emptied of all
but your art, but to your bench, your painting spot
alongside the Maumee, your family and I

gathered for the scattering. We shivered and sang
and said some words, Nels's shoulder a broad comfort
to lean against, and then his arm—swinging back
and forth—like a peasant sowing grain in a field.

"This is not him, but the box he came in," said Nick,
flinging the Not-you out from the shore. A larger bit
of grit pierced my palm in the fistful of you I held,
then tossed into mist. "Goodbye, darling," I told the air.

The river flowed slowly past and the clouds of you
spat on its surface, hissing like rain or fat on a skillet
as we stood there on that muddy ground, singing you up —
knock-knock-knockin' on Heaven's Door — casting you out
                                        into your stream.

Sun Hat: Cape Cod Photo #1

Here you are, squinting out from the straw hat
we bought at the Stop and Save,
and here I am, uncut, hair shaggier
than my dog's, its fringe a hinge of memory.

And what's a photo but a mirror,
one where I see you still seeing me
and meet again in your gaze the woman I was
the night we met, strangers just in from the rain.

Yellow Tornado Tree

Not like Monet, with his lilies and cool surfaces,
but your hazel eyes gazing into mine.
M. watched his wife's skin change color as breath left her body.
Close to the end now, you tell me "don't make too much"

of your hazel eyes gazing into mine,
but I yearn regardless for nuance and touch.
Close to the end now, you tell me "don't make too much"
of how much of life has passed us by,

but I yearn regardless for nuance and touch.
I recall your joy at your *Yellow Tornado Tree*,
not how much of life has passed us by.
"All I ever wanted" you told me: our lives lived as one.

How you laughed when you named it: *Yellow Tornado Tree*
with colors like swallows cascading up.
"All I ever wanted" you told me: our lives lived as one.
I will never forget your surprise

at how the yellows like swallows came cascading up.
Monet inspected Camille's skin as breath left her body.
I hold it close still, your wild surprise,
not like Monet, with his lilies and cool surfaces.

Dylan, Again

It was Bob Dylan in concert
at the Toledo Zoo that summer evening,
his voice almost beyond repair
as the sun set and the crowd sat
or stood, not quite filling the amphitheater.
Bob was wearing a yellow suit
with an array of Sgt. Pepper buttons—
a bellman's uniform, you called it.
You preferred Leon Russell
with his long white hair and beard
like a prophet come down
from the hills, and I agreed.
Then you yelled at the people
who stood and blocked our view,
shaking your fist in righteous rage.
I stayed still, my usual M.O.,
swallowing embarrassment.
Can't you think of it as so much gas,
Dr. Brodie said of your crankiness,
hot air—fingers waving in front
of her mouth—*that has to find its way out?*
Just let it go. And so I did. Darkness fell,
I took your arm, and there was Bob
stepping up to give us *Shelter from the Storm.*

Early Elegy

Of course, I know: it's time
to come to terms. You are ash, memory,
the grit and grain we scattered
from your painting spot onto the surface
of your beloved river, not far
from that small historic house
we came close to buying. Where I live now
I sit and look out from a three-season porch
much like the one you admired in Maumee.
You saw yourself making art there, grateful
for northern light from the un-curtained windows,
and sometimes I see you here, busy or laughing,
doing crosswords or finding new angles to sketch
among the rooftops and flower pots,
making ordinary days as ordinary people
who love one another are wont to do,
speculating about the breeze or the sky.

How You Left

I saw the Hairy Woodpecker
with its oddly yellow crown,
a bullfrog on the far side
of lily pads gleaming
in the sun, its throat a small balloon
and there were children beside us
peering into the woodland scene.
You gave each bird its one assignment:
this one scratching, that one peck-
pecking, and then just like that
they were gone. Not as if a door
opened or a human had walked out
into the feeder area.
Rather, it was circular,
some vortex had sucked them up.
I thought *waterspout, whirlwind.*
It got still. Then the hawk cried,
stretched wide its wings and landed.

Along Waite Road

as the sunset deepened
and blazed, I stopped to listen
into the dark stand
of barren trees
by the frozen
stream behind me
and heard as if from
another kingdom
an owl's soft, pulsing calls.
Despite cars rushing past
I heard it again, the song
on the verge of something
I could not name
but seemed to remember.
How could the sky be this fierce,
the woods so still, and you
not here beside me?

So Here

...you, by being dead, are more alive to me than ever.
– Alan Shapiro

So here I've gone and reframed your painting, the one of the
street with its tilted telephone poles, the street that led me
into sleep so often now bordered by an eggplant purple, very
trendy and advised by the decorator to pick up the purples
and greens of other pieces in my room, but it limits it now,
limits you, it's as if you are truly framed, captured, gone with
and within this frame. I should have chosen a lighter color,
a chalky off-white, something to move the eye outward, not
this dark lock. I still get lost in that street, the way I got lost
in the exhibit of Plains Indian Ledger Art yesterday, brought
up short by the bounding buffalo and sun dance memories
painted by Bear's Heart—shorn of his hair, imprisoned in
a fort in Florida—and then the blue-clad troops marching
his Cheyenne into a stockade, the warriors standing stiff,
two-dimensional against the gridded paper, heading into
an unthinkable dark. Oh, everywhere is doom and beauty,
ache and ruin, so it almost wasn't strange the way your
friend came up to me, surprised me in the act of looking and
brought you, as always, with him: your Van, a lifetime of
friendship and art and you there within it. Your paintings live
with me, bring me your voice, your antic laugh, your wry, sly
glances up from the surfaces of them. There you are working
at your easel in the corner of your studio, its tilted frame in
your lap, and there I am sitting in a chair across the room,
lifting my skirt.

Sometimes I think of us as children together, our stories intertwine. You were five, a young Diego filling your father's freshly painted wall, your crayons recreating the house fire from across the street, a red chaos billowing, sirens raging. I was seven when the teacher spoke to me sharply, so I turned over my paper and drew my home, the rocky drive, the house surrounded by woods, the slender pines that had fallen from snow and crossed my path so I could ride them like the horses I dreamed at night, the black one, the white one, flying me out into sleep among the stars.

Telling Time

Time rattles at our window/Time trying to get in.
– Minnie Bruce Pratt

You told time by the sun when you worked
En plein air you were your own challenger
Then adhering to your set-up rituals
The unzippering of the case of oil-
Pastels the unfolding of the easel
The tying it to a filled gallon jug
Lest wind pick up by the side of the road
Or else by the bridge over the Maumee
There in Sidecut Park off the main highway
After balancing the board on your lap
You'd stake out hours on the bench
On the bank to let the current or the leaves
Or your *divine selfishness* lead you
The sharpening light of evening always best
I could climb that the young woman announced
After she pulled off the road to take in
The smokestack of the abandoned Acme
Steam Plant rising magenta and orange
From your canvas—so now I know no place
Is too incongruous for love or sex
How the relentless rust of this region
Its nuclear plant slag heaps piles of salt
Dotting the industrial corridor
Between our towns could be worthy of love

It was all you ever wanted you told me
In the mauve twilight of the nursing home
Where I rushed every blessed chance I could
And when "draw" was all you could say
You took the marker from me and moved it
In permanent black lines across the white
Board and what started as a star became
A compass a clock something to parse
A lifetime with—a mechanical flower
That would collapse and devour you at last
Alone and afraid and me not there beside you.

A Blessing of Scallops: Eastern Market, Detroit

Sit. Feast on your life.

         – Derek Wolcott

Succulent pillows of salt and sea, flesh
dollops scooped from glistening shells, lined
across the Seafood Company's bed of ice—
can they tell me how waves know when to stop
cresting? If I walk alone through a midnight
graveyard, will my bones remain the same?
Maybe Brother Nature with his purslane,
arugula, and nasturtiums can explain why
the fox trotted through my yard in the middle
of yesterday or why the Pie Guy in the next stall
never seems to see me, even when I buy his apples
or admire his gooseberry pies. Cheese shop,
wine shop, backpack I stuff my groceries in
before crossing Gratiot and making my way
through the park and home to my love—or would,
except now I've moved far away and the market
is locked down, while across the planet Venice
has cancelled its yearly wedding with the sea.
No rings to toss to the waves now, so why
do I hear your voice in my dreams and why
did you call me in the middle of the night
months after you had died? *Dead, he is dead,*
I told the 2 a.m. voice on the line even though
I had just seen you sitting at my table,
watching me whisk a sauce for our scallops,
pen in your pocket protector, your shirt sleeves
rolled loosely above your finely boned wrists.

I know it's bad form

to write about dreams, but
Reader, I trust I won't lose you
when I say my love came to me
last night and we set out for
the river. I climbed onto my bike,
unridden since the spill that smashed
my ankle years before. He'd been
crippled, but moved along smoothly,
the lower half of his right leg
replaced by a bionic rod. He sped
ahead and soon was gone, but I
wobbled on and found him, sashaying
through traffic at a busy intersection.
It got quiet and we headed back
to his cluttered house.
    What he said to me then
disappeared with the dream,
but as we peered from his door down
through the piled up years of his art
I'm sure he heard me promise:
I'll come in and stay with you, I told him.

Sonny Rollins and the *redemptive handrail*

I keep on not knowing, and I cling to that like a redemptive handrail.
– Wislawa Szymborska

Take it...
    one note at a time, your breath the only constant
Except for there where sparrows drop below the line
    of the roof or where the rime-crusted grass you crunched
Over creates a little whine up your spine—Oh
    I want to be able to bear this, I've tried to—
To let it push out endlessly, the way a gong
    once sounded sends ripples into the universe
That never stop. Meanwhile one breath then another,
    mute then open, mull then recall—paths, canvases
Landscapes turned inside out, sun-bleached branches whitened
    against a black sky, slow pulsing slow slow darling
I loved you once the sax's moan reminds how down
    the sloping lawn or across the icy walk we
Held each other, grief's hushed joy now of a *purer*
    holier sort—this sad sweet feeling in the heart.
Still wading love's amber arpeggios I hear
    one chord's tingle replace the next then back, liquid
Tremolo rampant here vibrating nowhere's edge
    and I keep on not knowing, cannot say hand dog
Boot or glove outside or beyond only wonder
    if the moment cannot contain more sun than this.

Acknowledgments

I extend grateful acknowledgment to the editors of the following publications in which these poems first appeared:

Connecticut River Review "A Blessing of Scallops: Eastern Market, Detroit"
Dunes Review "At the National Gallery of Art: Memorial View"
Negative Capability "Early Elegy," "Yellow Tornado Tree"
Third Wednesday "How You Left," "Sun Hat: Cape Cod Photo #1"
One "Of Course" (as "Sanger, California")
Museum of Americana "Telling Time"
Maryland Literary Review "Maumee, Maumee"
Vox Populi "So Here"

Poems from this collection were finalists for *Cutthroat's* 2020 and 2021 Joy Harjo Poetry Prize.

"In Duple Time" borrows *you can't order a poem* from Naomi Shihab Nye's "A Valentine for Ernest Mann"—with thanks for her kind permission.

"Yellow Tornado Tree" received a Pushcart Prize nomination from *Negative Capability.*

In "Sonny Rollins and the *redemptive handrail,*" the line *I want to be able to bear this, I've tried to* was drawn from Orpheus's song in Ovid's *Metamorphoses* and the words *purer holier sort—this sad sweet feeling in the heart* from Abraham Lincoln's "Letter to Fanny McCullough."

Sincere gratitude also to the many friends in poetry whose voices live with me alongside these poems, especially Rhonda Green, Peter Markus, Judy Michaels, Diane DeCillis and the Quills, CT UU's in Prosetry, the MHFC's, the crew at Skazat!—with extra thanks to teachers *extraordinaire* Patrick Donnelly and Marie Howe for their precision and grace. To Jill Peek and Colin O'Brien, my endless appreciation for your steady guidance and aesthetic flair. And to Heidi Frankenhauser, much love always in memory of your dear Papa.

About the Author

TERRY BOHNHORST BLACKHAWK was born in California and grew up in Massachusetts, Georgia, and Indiana. As a student at Antioch College in the 1960s, she spent 18 months in Europe, learning both Swedish and Italian. After earning a BA in Literature, she moved to Detroit where her career as a high school Creative Writing teacher for Detroit Public Schools eventually led to her founding, in 1995, InsideOut Literary Arts Project, a nonprofit writers-in-schools program dedicated to amplifying the voices of Detroit youth. Blackhawk holds a Ph.D. in Reading and Language Arts Education from Oakland University, which granted her an Honorary Doctorate in 2013. Twice named Michigan Creative Writing Teacher of the Year, she has frequently shared her passions for ekphrastic poetry and for Emily Dickinson through poems, essays, workshops, and presentations. Her poetry collections include *body & field* (Michigan State UP, 1999); *Escape Artist* (BkMk Press, 2003) winner of the John Ciardi Prize; and *The Light Between* (Wayne State UP, 2012). *One Less River* (Mayapple Press) was named a Top 2019 Indie Poetry Title by *Kirkus Reviews*. Upon her retirement from InsideOut in 2015, Wayne State UP brought out *To Light a Fire: Twenty Years with the InsideOut Literary Arts Project*, a collection of essays co-edited with InsideOut Senior Writer Peter Markus. Other awards include the Pablo Neruda Prize for Poetry from *Nimrod International*, a Kresge Arts in Detroit Literary Fellowship, induction into the Michigan Women's Hall of Fame, and the Antioch College Horace Mann Alumni Award for victories for humanity. After fifty years as a Detroiter, Terry moved to Connecticut to live near her son, Yale Professor Ned Blackhawk, and grandchildren.